THE LIBRARY OF CONTEMPORARY THOUGHT

*America's most original voices
tackle today's most provocative issues*

EDWIN SCHLOSSBERG

INTERACTIVE EXCELLENCE
*Defining and Developing New Standards
for the Twenty-first Century*

"Gertrude Stein said that 'great art is irritation.' Mosquitoes irritate us, as do certain sounds and images. But does that make fingernails dragging across a blackboard art? Hardly. If something awakens us, moves us, transforms us, makes us feel and think in a new way, makes itself a part of us, that is a measure of greatness. Great art is what challenges us to see ourselves and each other more clearly. Great art makes us understand our relationship to the world we are in. Sometimes to change how we think we must look from a new perspective. Irritation *makes* us move away from our comfortable way of looking and our comfortable way of creating art. A movie like *The Graduate* or a book like *The Grapes of Wrath* stimulates us—irritates us, in a way—to become part of a new conversation, with others and within ourselves, about who, how, why, where, and when we are. . . ."

Also by Edwin Schlossberg

INTERACTIVE
EXCELLENCE

Defining and Developing New Standards for the Twenty-first Century

EDWIN SCHLOSSBERG

THE LIBRARY OF CONTEMPORARY THOUGHT
THE BALLANTINE PUBLISHING GROUP • NEW YORK

The Library of Contemporary Thought
Published by The Ballantine Publishing Group

Copyright © 1998 by Edwin Schlossberg

All rights reserved under International and Pan-American Copyright Conventions. Published in the United States by The Ballantine Publishing Group, a division of Random House, Inc., New York, and simultaneously in Canada by Random House of Canada Limited, Toronto.

http://www.randomhouse.com

Library of Congress Cataloging-in-Publication Data
Schlossberg, Edwin.
Interactive excellence : defining and developing new standards for the twenty-first century / by Edwin Schlossberg. — 1st ed.
p.   cm.
Includes bibliographical references.
ISBN 0-345-42371-2 (alk. paper)
1. Arts audiences—Psychology.   2. Arts—Public opinion.
I. Title.
NX220.S36   1998
700'.1'03—DC21   98-5104
CIP

Text design by Holly Johnson
Cover design by Ruth Ross
Cover art based on a photograph by Ross Muir

Manufactured in the United States of America

First Edition: July 1998

10   9   8   7   6   5   4   3   2   1

To Caroline, Rose, Tatiana, Jack,
and Peter

1

Educating the Audience—
and the Artist

WHEN ALEXANDER GRAHAM BELL invented the
telephone, he was unable to generate any
interest in using it. People could not imagine why
they would want or need to talk—immediately—
to someone who was across town or, even more
absurdly, in *another* town. Although people could
write letters to one another, and some could send
telegraph messages, the idea of sending one's voice
to another place then instantly hearing another
voice in return was simply not a model that existed
in people's experience. They also did not think it
was worth the money to accelerate sending or
hearing a message.

In frustration, and with the hope that if people
experienced something beautiful and exciting they

would realize they could not do without the telephone, Bell searched for a way to sell his concept.
He needed to create an audience.

To demonstrate the value of his invention, Bell
strung a telephone line between New York City
and Philadelphia, put telephones at a performance
of the Philadelphia Orchestra and at Town Hall in
New York, then invited people to come to Town
Hall to listen to the Philadelphia Orchestra through
the phone. He tried to make the medium of the
telephone serve as an extension of the theater. He
wanted the audience to experience the value of this
new kind of communication and used fine music
as the attraction. But the audience members were
only slightly amused: They were uninterested in
using Bell's new invention even after the extraordinary demonstration. Why? *They had not learned to
value immediate contact with distant people.*

The medium of the telephone and its place
in daily life could not be imagined by enough people. It took an acceleration in the events of daily
life—accomplished by the simultaneous introduction of electricity in most homes and the affordable
automobile—to create a context in which people
thought immediate conversations would be useful.

In more recent times, the people who introduced the fax machine experienced the same lack

of interest in their product until Federal Express familiarized people with the pleasure of nearly immediate document transfer. Once people had the experience of receiving documents overnight, the usefulness of having them even more immediately caught on. And since the cost to do this was not prohibitive, faxing took off—after twenty years of languishing sales.

Here's an easy fact to understand: Audiences are slow to change with the introduction of new technology.

Here's a much more difficult fact to grasp: Educating the audience to be able to fully use and appreciate new technology is often the *last* thing inventors consider. Even being aware that an education process is *needed* is usually not in inventors' minds as they rush to share their new creations.

EVER SINCE I WAS a child I have been as interested in the audience as I am in the show. At any event I went to, I was curious why people had decided to come, what they were thinking, how they'd discuss what was seen. I wondered what their education was and what they had in common with other members of the audience. What books, what movies, what images, were central to their experience? I wondered if they had a preconceived idea of their experience and how they would compare what *was* happening to what they *thought* might happen. If a play was about a segment of society—the homeless, let's say, or the very rich—or a place or period of time—Shakespeare's England or Molière's France or Jules Verne's future—of which they were not a part, did the audience feel like outsiders? Was the moral center of the play taken to heart? Did they think of themselves as participants—critics or actors or writers—or merely observers?

My interest in audiences was and is not just in those who go to formal plays or opera or dance. The audience has always been, for me, readers of books, listeners to music, visitors to a store, patrons of an art gallery, museum, zoo, or sports event, and now, in our increasingly media-dominated times, witnesses to a celebrity event—an event at which people are celebrated for their fame rather than for their accomplishments.

How does an audience assemble from various parts of a society? What are the means by which an audience is signaled that this book, movie, or event is for them? Why does an audience pay attention to a performance? What is it that encourages individuals and groups to allocate time and resources to an event or to a work of art? How and why does the audience continue paying attention, and what makes them stop? What signals determine the relationship that will or will not exist with the work of art? Thinking about these issues is crucial to understanding the way a culture proceeds.

On the surface this might sound as if I am talking about market research or analysis. Not really. I am interested in the patterns and forces that shape and create a culture. I am not interested in learning how to subvert the interest of an audience into things that are for sale or create methods for propaganda. What I am interested in is calling attention to the discipline of looking at the audience as *part* of the act of composition or design.

Market research or market analysis simply tries to understand ways to enlarge the audience. The increase in the size of an audience is irrelevant to creating an exciting, interested, and involved audience. The conversation that exists between members of an audience about what they are experiencing, and the conversation that exists through the audience as a whole, is the substance of our culture. Our culture *exists* in these conversations. Realizing not only that these conversations are occurring but that they should be consciously included in the consideration of a design or composition is central to my interest in writing and creating environments. Understanding how the relationship between the audience and the performance creates the culture is crucial to the development of a great culture.

OF COURSE, WITHOUT A show there can be no audience, and without an audience there can be no conversation. So I am equally interested in the things audiences experience: the books, poems, plays; the museums, zoos, stores; the art. I am intrigued by the relationship between how audiences develop and how things are made for and with these audiences. Measures of popularity and measures of excellence are established by this relationship. Excellence often precedes popularity and is often defined by a smaller audience, one that is contemporary with the creation of the cultural work or artifact. Popularity can be the measure of excellence, but it also can be the result of marketing or other factors. Things that are popular seem to fly in the face of the definition of excellence, and vice versa.

The important issue is that excellence is not to be considered as something that resides only in the work itself. Excellence, like popularity, is defined by its relationship with its audience. It is the audience in relationship with the artist that creates standards of excellence. Such standards serve as guideposts for each generation, leading them toward the most interesting and important ideas that must be considered. Standards of excellence also serve as means by which to measure the quality and the purpose of the society at large and, in comparison, the culture.

The process of establishing standards of excellence is fraught with examples of corruption as well as stories of inspiration. What is critical is that the entire process of creating, admiring, and learning from artists and audiences become a conscious and intentional effort. Complaining about the loss of standards, the inferior quality of works of art, or the poor quality of an audience only reinforces the need to consider all of these aspects in the plans to understand or change the nature of the cultural process.

WHEN I WAS EIGHT years old, a friend of my parents gave me a kit to build a small ham radio. After building it, I turned it on and tuned it, and suddenly there were all these people talking. When I thanked the friend for the gift, I asked her how she had arranged for all the other people to be out there to talk to. She laughed and said she had not arranged for them, she had simply bought the kit. "Well, why are they talking?" I asked. She said, probably just to quiet me, "Go find out." Over the past twenty years I have been finding out.

Building that radio, like building a theater or museum, is great, but it becomes meaningful only through the interaction between people. Conversations create a culture and sustain it. It is not the static on the radio that is interesting, but the quality of the engagement between people using words, music, or sounds that makes the experience important. The subject, the content, the artistic mode, can vary, but being engaged in the conversation is what it is all about. And once engaged, you have to evaluate what you and others think about what you are seeing: Is it interesting or entertaining or bad enough to make you leave? Standards of excellence help to provide a measure against which to compare the things you hear, see, and feel.

There are many reasons that our standards change: New artists and new audiences are enfranchised by access to new media; there are economic and educational shifts in society; and just because of the weather of life. In this century there have been some dramatic changes in many art forms. In music, the romantic classical standards of the music of Brahms, for example, have been challenged by the atonal and random music of a composer such as Igor Stravinsky or Morton Feldman. In painting, the more representational works of Manet or Winslow Homer have been challenged by expressionistic work of painters such as Jackson Pollock or Robert Motherwell, which seeks to show the process of painting as the subject of the work. In literature, the standards of excellence measured by chronologically accurate stories of people's lives were challenged by writers who disregarded the conventions of storytelling and created evocative narratives that are independent of time or place, such as the works of James Joyce or Virginia Woolf.

As each of these art forms has developed, the standards of excellence have changed, because one or more artists have broken new ground and have communicated in a way that excites and interests a small audience. If the audience grows and in the process explains to others the values of the new works, the artist and the work begin to define a new standard of excellence. The audience becomes part of the artist's work, and the appreciation, criticism, and discussion of the work creates its place in the culture.

Standards have also changed dramatically as the size of the population has expanded and the tools to communicate between artist and audience have increased in scope and reliability. Excellence, which used to be determined by a few people within the small population that was interested, is now created by a vast network of artists, producers, all the people who operate the media, and a gigantic audience. The audience is enlarging because of access to forums on the Internet and public access television, where they can express their ideas. This is just the beginning of the establishment of local "electronic neighborhoods" that extend and enhance the dynamic role of audiences in the creation of culture and society.

In 1900, there were approximately 75 million people in the United States. Seven thousand or so books were published that year. Now there are about 275 million people in the United States, and more than fifty thousand new books are published every year. Almost every home in America has a television set; most have videocassette players; and about a third have computers. That means the vast majority of Americans have access in their homes to cultural events that once could occur only in a hall or theater.

The audience for *everything* has grown in size, and the number of experiences to watch has grown even more rapidly. These two factors mean that the *nature* of the audience must change. When that occurs, our current standards of excellence must be rethought and redefined. New standards our grandparents could not have imagined need to be developed. Without a method to properly evaluate excellence, our huge and growing population cannot learn or develop effectively, because learning occurs only when conversations, ideals, and goals have a shared and understandable framework.

For example, people often evaluate the conversations in chat rooms on the Internet from the perspective of whether they are informative and accurate or even if they are good debate. The fact is, chat rooms are just like talk on the front stoop or over the backyard fence and should be seen as such. But because they are on a technological medium, the evaluation of what is carried is measured from a more sophisticated perspective.

The good news is that these new, nonhierarchical tools of the Internet and the interactive tools available in public places can provide a framework for creating new evaluative tools. But for that framework to succeed, our society, government, and corporations must support it. More important, perhaps, the audience itself must understand the power it has to shape, develop, and share in our society's creations.

2

Changes in Technology Create New Audiences

M AKING SOMETHING CERTAINLY IMPLIES that someone has considered a use for it, right? And creating a cultural artifact or event *definitely* implies that someone has thought about whether or not an audience exists for that particular thing, doesn't it? The answer to both questions is a resounding no. So *many* things are made before their use is established or before their audience is understood. This detachment is not necessarily a bad thing, however. Yes, it can be a problem, but it can also be a source of greatness. Inventors, artists, and writers create for an imagined audience. Sometimes they are right, and a large audience immediately finds and appreciates their work. But sometimes it takes a huge effort and a long time before any conversation between the work and its audience is ever established.

It is hard for us to imagine people thinking that the telephone is not an obvious and important tool in the conduct of daily life. But it was not considered important until the speed of daily life increased. Now think about the way that the computer is regarded. Computers have really only entered into most people's lives in the past four or five years, and they are still mostly used for writing. The idea that it is a communication tool that might actually replace mail, or a tool of information access that might, with the aid of the Internet, eventually replace libraries, is still an awkward and unappealing concept for most people. A tool is *often* invented before its main use is understood. Then, once the invention is in place, technological advances pressure the audiences to invent or adopt uses for it. The Internet itself was invented to enable scientists at universities to exchange information. It was only when a software package was invented that made access easy and free that many people realized the opportunity that the Internet provided.

Audiences make a technology great, and audiences always need to adapt the way they are doing things in order to fully work with the new technology. People learn how to talk on the telephone and how to organize their lives to optimize its use, but it takes time for this to happen.

WHEN I THINK TO make something, I try to imagine how all different groups in the audience will actually experience what I make. Often the audience develops an interesting and surprising use that I did not consider. At Macomber Farm, a museum/farm/park that I designed, there was an exhibit where people could compare their stride to the stride of a horse. The people were on a treadmill that had a television camera focused on it. That image was shown alongside an image of a horse running. Most people enjoyed trying to be as graceful as the horse. But some people teamed up—one person took the role of the front legs and the other the back legs, to see if together they could run like a horse—a behavior I never anticipated.

I also try to understand what each individual

and each small group will consider to be their role during the experience—how they will learn or have fun experiencing the content and the design.

For any idea to be understood, it must be presented so that the audience can recognize a model of it in their mind. The model can be assembled from previous associations—for example, the audience must know the game of baseball to understand a story based on that sport, or they must be familiar with how airplanes fly to appreciate an action story with lots of airplanes—but the model must be there, or else no understanding can happen. The talking and joking or even the quick exchange of looks between members of an audience is crucial to the success of an experience. The overall ambience of an audience and how it reacts is complemented by the conversation in each smaller group and between individuals.

The interaction between the reader and the book, the visitor and the museum, is to me a new experiment every single time. For example, at Macomber Farm, I also designed binocularlike devices that replicated the optical structure of the eyes of every farm animal. My experiment allowed the visitors to look at the world through the eyes of a particular animal and understand more about that animal. But it had never been done before, so I did not know whether the audience would relate to the experience or find it impossible to understand. I didn't even know if they would accept the process itself. Getting the audience to participate is, of course, a necessary first step in any experiment and interaction. So, in this instance, I put humorous phrases on the devices—things like "I am seeing like a cow"—to signal that this was not a *serious* experiment and that they should not be embarrassed to try the binoculars on. Humor can be an important welcoming device and can ease the strain of the experiment on the audience. There is *always* a strain on the audience when experiencing something new, because they are not sure what they can do or whether they will be embarrassed for not doing it right. Therefore, in a public facility the design must anticipate a wary public, even if the experience is simply an attempt to educate or amuse.

PUBLIC EVENTS ARE TOO often seen as large-scale presentations, speeches, or demonstrations. In fact, they are opportunities for the public to learn from each other as well as from the performance. When that interaction occurs, not only can the audience properly experience the presented material, it can also sense itself as being part of an interesting community. Unfortunately, that balance is a rare occurrence—because neither the audience nor the artist/presenter is used to looking at the presentation in this way. Audiences are usually not encouraged to converse among themselves. I am not suggesting that people should be talking during a theatrical performance. But I *am* suggesting that the focus of attention that is usually directed toward the work presented and not toward enabling the audience to experience the work by discussing anything about it be reconsidered.

If the experience at a public event does not enable members of the audience to learn from one another, and if each member of society is increasingly isolated because he or she is getting most cultural events at home, there are no opportunities for the audience members to improve their ability to appreciate one another as well as the works presented. This is why audiences are not getting better *as audiences*. This lack of awareness about the audience has consequences for our society that are worrisome and could be dangerous. There is a hunger for community, and if it is not encouraged to grow, some demonic leader could capitalize on the sense of anomie and alienation that isolation causes.

THE RELATIONSHIP BETWEEN THE audience and the artist sets a tone that can make communication either easy or difficult. One of the things Buckminster Fuller is remembered for today is his inspiring lectures. At those lectures, many of which I attended, he helped the audience to understand some of the problems that were occurring around the earth. Fuller also used to tell his audience that it was *their* responsibility to *act* on those problems, but he gave no guidance as to what they should do. As a result, many people left Fuller's lectures feeling excited but impotent. When people are excited by a lecturer, they also need to be helped to understand how to translate that excitement into action. This is the measure of a great lecturer. One has to speak with an understanding of what the audience knows and can accept. It is also crucial to consider what can be done to enable audience members to learn from one another, not just from the composer/speaker/artist. That is the only way to create a new context for audience excellence to develop.

Marshall McLuhan's work directs attention to the tension between the audience and the artist. He also expands that tension to include the effect of tools. According to McLuhan, the lightbulb and the printing press have affected culture more than the content illuminated on the page. Because the lightbulb made reading possible for all the hours of every day, it made reading much more prevalent and, as a result, more important throughout the society. Because of the printing press, ideas and culture and access to understanding became possible for anyone who could read. That, too, made reading more attractive and made it a more desirable skill for everyone. These inventions helped to blur the distinctions of power and class. It is McLuhan's premise that the mere *content* of a book would never have had this level of an effect. McLuhan is suggesting that the construction of the context of communication— the building of the theater—precedes any impact that the content could have and is more important than any relationship that can develop between artist and audience. This makes perfect sense . . . to an extent.

There can be no dynamic relationship between

the audience and the artist until there is a context in which this conversation can take place. The construction of the context, of the medium, precedes the effect the content can have. The medium does control the message insofar as it becomes the means to communicate it. But once the medium exists, it is the relationship between the message and the receiver that is crucial. McLuhan's insistence on consciously watching the effects of context has had a very important effect on cultural thinking. It has made people more aware of how the media delivers its message and has helped people to focus on the appropriateness of a particular medium for a given content. By making people aware of the contribution of context, McLuhan made it easier to evaluate both context and audience in relation to a work.

Building on this idea of context, the theater works well as a metaphor when thinking about communications: Someone has something to say, the theater serves as the context for it, and the audience is the listener. It is a simple way to keep the roles straight when trying to analyze the issues that need to be thought about. For example, now that people are presenting material on the Internet, the "theater" is the Internet/telephone/computer.

Communications technology, such as the telephone, has historically connected one person to another. Now, with television and the Internet, one person can talk to thousands, even millions. This change of context has affected not only the means of communication but the actual way we communicate. There are people who are good at talking to one person only, some who can talk to small groups, some who are good with larger groups, and so on. Great politicians and orators can and do hold hundreds, thousands, sometimes millions in their sway.

As radio, television, and film entered our culture, the physical theater—the context in which messages are delivered—changed dramatically. Because a huge amphitheater is very different from your living room, the presentation and the style of public address have changed. Once, when people stood in a square and heard a powerful address, they could feel the rest of the audience being moved by what was said. Now, alone in your living room, you can't know if what is being said affects only you or is moving to many. You are being *spoken* to as if you are a member of a crowd, but you can't get any sense of the effect these words have on the crowd. You are forced to listen, and you must trust the voices appearing on the medium itself, since you can hear no other voices.

This has created a more passive audience, one that cannot differentiate between voices whose purpose is to hype or sell and voices that are truly engaging their audience in a meaningful dialogue. The danger is that people will take the hype as meaningful and that the meaningful message will be confused with hype.

SEVERAL YEARS AGO IN Indonesia, I attended a performance of the shadow puppet theater known as *wayang kulit,* and I was overwhelmed by an entirely new audience/theater/artist paradigm.

The story told in the *wayang kulit* performance is always based on one of the Hindu classics, such as the Ramayana or the Mahabharata, with which the audience is familiar. Because the audience knows the story before going in, it is primarily interested in comparing this performance to previous ones. The performance, which lasts eight hours, begins around midnight on the night of the full moon. Throughout the entire performance and then afterward, the audience quietly chats about the show—how it is going and how it went. The whole experience is a way for the community to get together and have a shared experience.

Before the show I sat down in the front of the *kraton*, the king's palace, and saw a large white curtain, like a makeshift movie screen, strung across the middle of a platform. A strong lamp hung in what I thought was the backstage area. The *gamelan* musicians sat in what I perceived to be the front, with the shadow from the puppets projected on the white cloth. As the performance started, some of the audience sat in the front and watched the shadows dance. But others got up and moved *behind* the stage to watch the puppeteer and the puppets. One part of the audience chose to step into illusion, listening and watching from the front, while the other part chose to be with the performer, to explore the art of his presentation. This practice, so alien to Western tradition, allows the audience to learn how something is made and how well it can be done. Their understanding, discussion, and appreciation of *all* facets of the play are part of the presentation. The culture values the audience's active role in the process as equal in importance to that of the puppeteer or musician. A performance is considered from all these points of view, not simply on the basis of the performance alone.

In Western theater, we do not want to break the illusion. We want the actor, director, and writer to be invisible, and we, as the audience, want to remain passive observers of their art. The Western audience acts—and is thought of—as a single group that shares an experience of illusion. Except in the case of highly experimental theater, any audience awareness of the process that creates the illusion has usually been considered a failure of that process. This is taken to extremes in the tone poem *Till Eulenspiegel,* where the main character breaks the illusion during a performance and the audience kills him—a tad harsh as a reaction, but true to our desire to keep the audience totally separate from the process of telling the story.

WHEN MEMBERS OF AN audience can sense one another's presence or can talk to one another about the thing that is seen, this is, *to a degree,* an interactive experience. When an audience begins to participate in conversations with—to stay with the theater metaphor—the playwright, as is happening in Internet chat rooms, and when the experience of an event happens both *in front* of the audience and *between* its members, this creates a whole new paradigm. It is also the best way I know to define a *truly* interactive experience. However, standards of excellence for interactive experience are not so easily defined. To be understood, they must be shown through examples rather than merely described.

3

Standards of Excellence Reveal
the Nature of the Audience

WHAT IS IT THAT makes something culturally valuable and therefore considered excellent? Every culture worldwide has developed some objective standards of excellence so that they can identify the best dancer, composer, book, or speaker rather than leaving it to a personal criterion of excellence. Popular culture includes those works that are measured only by their ability to draw crowds. Popular culture contains works that usually aspire not to challenge but to express only those themes and stories that are common to the broadest possible audience.

Historically, most cultures select what is excellent with guidance from the most educated and often the elite. Having objective criteria for excellence provides incentives for young, aspiring artists, provides rewards for the talented, and helps the majority decide what is worthy of their time and attention. Resources in the past were limited, so fewer artworks were created, and, as a result, the number of people and creations that were deemed excellent were few. As resources have increased and channels of presentation have exploded—first radio, then television, and now the Internet—the opportunity to present more creations has also increased. Unquestionably, this has contributed to the erosion of the standards of excellence, often to the point of inclusion of solely popular works into the category of excellent work. Standards have changed to reflect a less educated audience and therefore an audience that does not yet understand some of the issues that are being discussed and presented to them.

In the past, the programs of serious orchestras would never have included the work of John Philip Sousa. The list of serious works in the theater would not have included the work of Andrew Lloyd Webber. And the work of LeRoy Neiman would not have been included in the collection of a major museum. These are works that are sold to the audience and do not contain contentious, disturbing, or serious problems, or any suggestion of the need for solutions. They are popular because they do *not* do this and because they present a contained, well-understood, shared view of the world. They do not point to any new ideas or new ways to deal with old ideas.

But we, as a technological culture, are in a transitional stage, and that transition gives us a rare and wonderful opportunity. The increase in audience size and the increase in the number of contexts for presentation provide an opportunity for the audience to become better educated and, in turn, gradually develop their *own* new standards of excellence. The issue is about *not* limiting what is shown. It is pointless to bemoan that popular works do not aspire to change the structures of society. The issue is to become aware that the opportunity to communicate with larger, different, and changing audiences is now greater than ever. The issue is that communication must focus not only on the work but on the development of a relationship between the work and the audience.

Evaluation of excellence is a necessary responsibility that we all take on when we become part of a culture. Part of the improvement of a culture depends on the audience's ability to learn how to evaluate what they have seen and how to express their conclusion. Having a broad choice of critics who can express ideas that are understood by varied audiences helps enormously. Between 1900 and 1950, when the Broadway theater was in its prime, there were always at least eight different New York theater critics writing in eight different newspapers. The audience could choose which critic and criticism worked for them. It also helped to have performances that were good. Because of the criticism, as well as other factors— theater did not have television to compete with, so interest in the theater was higher—the shows seemed to get better. Having a good critical environment helps to place the audience in the experience; it asks the audience to evaluate both the play and its relationship to it. Audiences that develop standards of excellence can become better at understanding that the experience *includes* them. Without awareness of this, the quality of the experience often deteriorates.

For many years, opera was broadcast on radio along with commentary and explanation paralleling a performance. This extended and enhanced the audience by making the experience less forbidding to those who did not already understand what the opera was and what stories it told. In the future, performances can be even further extended and enhanced using the Internet. People can have a discussion about the opera and a particular performance. Each member of the opera audience can be given the chance to express an opinion, discuss the performance with other members of the audience, and get feedback about his or her own understanding and appreciation. As in the *wayang kulit*, instead of lowering the standards of performance, this provides access to the history of the opera as well as extending the role of an informed and active audience.

GERTRUDE STEIN SAID THAT "great art is irritation." Mosquitoes irritate us, as do certain sounds and images. But does that make fingernails dragging across a blackboard art? Hardly. If something awakens us, moves us, transforms us, makes us feel and think in a new way, makes itself a part of us, that is a measure of greatness. Great art is what challenges us to see ourselves and each other more clearly. Great art makes us understand our relationship to the world we are in. Sometimes to change how we think we must look from a new perspective. Irritation *makes* us move away from our comfortable way of looking and our comfortable way of creating art. A movie like *The Graduate* or a book like *The Grapes of Wrath* stimulates us—irritates us, in a way—to become part of a new conversation, with others and within ourselves, about who, how, why, where, and when we are.

The sociologist Edward Carpenter quoted a Balinese villager as saying, "We have no art. We do everything as well as possible." In Bali the role of art is to help create and sustain a nonhierarchical culture—a culture in which there is no hierarchical difference between the audience and the actor. The theater of the Balinese is the world itself, enlarged by their communal ability to share with each other their skills and realize that a cultural event is the work of everyone—audience, actor, singer, and those who build the stage. Everyone contributes his or her skill to the overall production, and no one has a higher position within the culture for what he or she contributes.

In modern Western culture, art serves a completely different purpose. It is a way to see into parts of our world that most of us cannot or do not look at or see. Western culture has always thought of art as an object that is a focus of harmony and beauty to which we could all aspire; we have resisted the idea of art as irritation. We have thought of the arts as conveyors of learning, attaching what we have learned to a specific form in order to preserve it for future generations. But the tools with which we present art have changed. To take the McLuhanesque view, when context changes, the audience must change, too. And when that happens, art itself is going to change. To *accept* these changes, we must continue to experience and appreciate art as it develops. To move forward artistically as a culture, we need to further expand our tolerance, to appreciate the way an artist weaves his or her presentation in and amongst the audience and the way the audience becomes more active in that experience. To improve as an audience, we must engage ourselves in experiences that are both beautiful *and* irritating.

4

The Tools of Communication
Change the Conversation

W ITH NEW TOOLS OF communication and context such as television and the Internet, art can again—as after the printing press or the lightbulb—provide an opportunity to explore new standards and new lessons on a much broader level than ever before. When the tools of communication connected only one person to another, there was no mass culture. But as new forms of communication were developed—radio, television, movies, the Internet—more people were included and wanted to be included in the audience. Broadcasters needed to expand the audience as the audience wanted what the broadcasters provided. For the mass audience, media had to become huge to be successful—and its sheer size made it difficult to consider carrying complex messages that would be appropriate only to small audiences. Mass culture, especially television, whose entertainment programming exists to advocate and to sell products and thus must appeal to the broadest possible audience at all times, demands basic and simple messages that everyone can understand.

Even though these messages need to be broadly welcoming and inviting, they can also help us to become a better audience. The challenge for artists and producers in the mass media is to entertain us without being bland and unadventurous. Popular culture can bring us closer together by presenting stories that show shared values and shared goals that subtly challenge us to become more fully realized as people, as families, and as a society. To that end, the audience needs to be considered an essential part of any composition, even if that composition is intended for popular entertainment.

When a television is on in our house, we are linked to a huge culture, some parts of which are important for us to watch or be entertained by and some of which are not. We need to learn to be able to sort through the ever-increasing array. We now believe that if an event of major proportions happens anywhere in the world, we will hear about it—instantly. We now think that television provides a way for us to have the choice and the ability to look into anything and everything that is interesting. Television can be a window onto the world, and, as the huge number of people who watch television demonstrates, we are definitely interested in that world. But to get the full picture we must learn to examine many different and sometimes conflicting media.

Television makes us passive observers of the world rather than active participants in it. The sense that television provides the unique stage on which the standards of a culture occur creates a dissonance with reality and can cause a withdrawal from immediate communal activities. That can contribute to the erosion of the physical life of cities. Not long ago, there was no choice of what to do in the evening or on the weekend but spend time with others in one's neighborhood. The local basketball court or park or church was a required object of attention, since everyone shared its benefits. When entertainment moved into the living room, the sense of shared experience was replaced by *imagined* shared experience, and the sense of responsibility for local facilities disappeared.

Because television is not directed toward conversation in the room between viewers or family members, it can also waste valuable family time. Because most parents work, the opportunity to learn along with children, the chance to role-play and exchange ideas and jokes, occurs only during evenings and weekends. Few families have the resources or skills to compete with television programming that tells stories without the need for any participation. Thus, precious time that could be used to build family experiences and learn together passes without any communication or interaction occurring.

Since culture depends on communication, most older cultures were local, subject only to the intrusion of commerce or war. Improvements to communication and transportation changed this; when electronic communications began to spread, local cultures were threatened. Movies introduced new realities to the world, and the movie stars became imaginary members of the community. Radio was different, because it introduced voices from distant places and reported on things happening worlds away. People still knew more about local events than they did about national and world events until 1941, when President Roosevelt told everyone about the attack on Pearl Harbor. From that moment, the nation and the world were in everyone's living room.

Mass culture has been a product of the combination of all the current media—radio, television, national magazines, national newspapers. Before mass culture arrived in the 1950s, the smaller, local communication tools, mainly newspapers and radio, provided the publisher and broadcaster an exclusive forum for their dominant voice—and that voice had the ability to set the standards for excellence and opinion. As electronic media expanded from local stations to the entire country and then the world, the audience only had to pay for the electricity, and later the cable fees, to have the television and radio on all the time. One dominant voice disappeared; suddenly there were *many* voices. The audience was able to choose what appealed to them from a wide array, and the programming started to have to chase the audience. In their own living rooms, the audience tuned in to things that were most like themselves, things that most fit in with their world. Voices and channels began to shape their messages to best fit this new world of smaller, more defined audiences. The voices in the mass media began to be very personal. They presented society with issues that affect and reflect *everyone*—not just the elite. Unlike the old culture, the new mass culture is a mirror, not a window. It is sustained by being present and *turned on* in as many homes as possible, like the lightbulb. The competition between the channels is for audience size and not, as in the past, for control through development of ideas or significant issues.

Mass communication tools invent a common-denominator culture. This creates a subtle climate of anxiety for everyone, because it fully satisfies no one—neither those who watch and express no opinion, nor those who have an opinion but cannot get it heard. In today's mass culture, those who have been more highly educated and still maintain an interest in the hierarchical ideas, standards, and beliefs of the previous elite feel that standards have declined, even disappeared. Those who never learned these standards (or who aspire to become the voice of dominance) want their *own* standards to replace the dominant one. Those who aspire to become the dominant arbiters of taste will find that when filtered through the mass media, their voice becomes weaker—it becomes part of the simplified whole, a whole that reflects few interesting or challenging ideas. (Think of a political campaign where important concepts are reduced to sound bites.) Eventually these new aspirants to positions of cultural dominance, such as Pat Robertson, open their own channels and fight to reach an audience. Robertson's odyssey from minister to spokesperson for the religious right, to presidential candidate, to television magnate, and finally to talk show host depicts how the media transforms a small voice into a large one, but one that no longer contains much of its original concerns.

Forty years ago, you knew that your community—the friends and associates in your life who were part of your neighborhood or town, who worked with you or participated in local institutions—was watching the same popular television shows you watched. People of *all* ages watched Ed Sullivan, Jack Benny, and Milton Berle, usually as a family. Today, interest in popular entertainment is not as much a common experience as it used to be—except for men watching sports and children watching everything. Children, because of school, are now the only members of a local community who meet daily. As a result, aside from the sports audience, they have become the most marketable audience for programming on television. The objective of marketing is to create perceived value in an object. But perceived value only works as a currency in a community where the perception can be shared. Therefore, children at school every day fulfill both objectives. They can absorb the marketing and have a forum to show off their purchases.

There are now so many more choices of programs, and many homes have more than one television, so family members do not watch the same show. By creating separate audiences, television has actually changed the concept of what a family is. It is no longer the smallest unit of a community with common interests even for what is on television. That makes the growth of family conversations and interplay even more difficult. A family was the center of feelings of love, the center of establishing values, of creating aspirations for the future. When each member of the family is getting different messages and models of what the world is about, and when family time is absorbed in getting these messages, the family has little time or resources to realize its purpose.

Television is also the dominant advertising medium of our times. Cultural values have gotten merged with and expressed through products. When advertising uses the tools of art, film, and theater to engage us, then the experience of the product becomes the expression of the culture that we are.

Wearing Nike sneakers or a Timberland jacket conveys that the wearer is part of a certain segment of the culture. The desire for community has been redirected through television. We have become an evanescent community of consumers and watchers rather than a dynamic audience whose members learn from each other. Not only is this unsatisfying and stultifying, it is a most dangerous trend: Sneakers are sneakers; they don't talk or have feelings, and retreating into a world of products denies each of us the struggles and successes that go along with living in an interdependent community.

A RTISTICALLY, THE CULTURE NEEDS to be refreshed in ways that television cannot accomplish. In India there is a Hindi word, *raunag,* that means the pleasure of being in crowds. Needless to say, we do not have such a word in our vocabulary. In a strange paradox of our culture, we have long equated crowds with discomfort, despite the fact that we are all drawn to things that others like and can share in. We need to complement one rich tradition, the power of the individual, with another rich tradition, the importance of working with, learning from, and enjoying the presence of large groups. The more the world is connected via modern communication tools, the more important it becomes to heal this inherent split in our cultural personality.

With the advent of a tool as powerful as the Internet, the need for historical perspective and the ability to determine quality and excellence become ever more important. Recently, Western culture seems to have become unfamiliar with its own artifacts, ideas, and tools. Tests among American high-school students, for example, show that they neither know about nor *want* to know about U.S. history. It is as if we are transforming ourselves so rapidly that any historical artifact or message is perceived as an obstacle rather than a means toward understanding. Yet the Internet, with its large academic, scientific, and governmental databases, provides a decentralized data bank and mass-distribution channel that gives this same audience that is uninterested in the past more access to it.

What we have never fully taken advantage of is the fact that each of the mass communication tools available to us provides information and access to information in radically different ways. Each of these tools has strengths that are derived from where we see them and the quality and kind of information that they can carry. We have never been able to choose how to use each of these media before, since their combined presence is new. And with changes in technology happening constantly, this picture will continue to change. But it is interesting to look at some of their strengths and consider whether we can redirect our messages and performances differently to enhance the experience and development of the culture.

Print, both newspapers and books, provides the most effective way to present information that we must rely on. Because it is stable and can be copied and compared, print is the medium that provides the information of record. It is also the medium that, at present, provides the most inexpensive portable way to distribute data.

Radio provides the best way to engage the intellect and the emotions simultaneously. Because it is invisible and seems to come from everywhere, radio appeals to memory and to emotions and therefore is perfect for music, stories, and gossip. Since it does not require conscious attention, it is also good for getting weather and news while working or traveling.

The telephone provides the connection between all members of a society and, more important, the connection to each person's community. It is the means to provide an extended experience of community created by the ease and low cost of transportation.

Museums and large public attractions provide ways to create conversations about moments in the past, present, and future, and about ideas in any discipline. They provide the experiential base through which members of a society, at various levels of sophistication, can become part of the conversations about what is important.

Theater provides the most effective way to communicate the ideas and principles of society and the most immediate way to challenge and experience what is considered funny, important, horrifying, and so on. Theater is a way for an audience to find out what feelings are shared or not shared with most people.

Movies provide extraordinary ways to summarize and understand change. They are like print in that they are a medium of record, but because they can be altered and changed, animated and adapted, they are the record of the imagination as well as the event. They collapse and focus experiences, stories, and even whole epochs into performances that can be explored. They are the best vehicles to present and review ideas of history and plans for the future. Also, because of the scale of films, they enable us to disconnect from our present life and play the role of the composer with the director and filmmaker and the audience.

Broadcast television is the means to provide a general connection to each of us from other parts of the society and the world. It is the medium of the present moment. But sometimes the technology is confused with the process of broadcast. The television technology can also be used as a small movie screen, or display for computer output, and more recently as a monitor for viewing the Internet.

Each of the mass communication tools will be linked in some way in the next decades to create new communication experiences. The only way that we can effectively orchestrate this development is by becoming more connected with different-scale communities around us. These can be actual physical neighborhoods, virtual electronic neighborhoods, or groups that assemble from work or from interests or from beliefs. The important issue is that by democratizing access to information and to the forums for discussion and presentation, everyone becomes responsible for what and how he communicates and how he participates in the society and in the cultures of his choosing. It creates a need for communication, participation, and responsibility unparalleled in human history.

5

New Standards of Excellence
Are Needed

A S PART OF A *60 Minutes* story about the 1996 crash of TWA Flight 800, Lesley Stahl interviewed a man who had posted on his website hundreds of pages about his opinions of how and why the plane exploded and crashed. During the interview she interrupted him to say, "Excuse me, but it seems that you have made up all this information. You haven't done any research; you don't know if anything you say is truth or rumor or malicious speculation." To which he responded: "So? . . . If people don't want to believe it, they can go to another website."

Can they? Yes, absolutely. But the fear is that they won't.

We always have the fear that any lie perpetrated via a cultural medium will influence the less educated and the more impressionable. We worry that this guy's voice will be equated with legitimate sources of news and information. But as channels of communication increase nearly exponentially, and more dubious voices are presented, the public must search further, and work harder, and scrutinize more closely to find the voices they trust. It places more responsibility on the audience. That responsibility must eventually lead to knowledge, and that knowledge means that reliable sources may be more closely scrutinized than ever before if our society becomes more able and conscious of its responsibilities. It is not inevitable, but if it happens, that should make some sources even more reliable and thus more important.

THE STANDARDS OF TRUTH and responsibility are now perceived as variable because of the overwhelming amount of material that is being made available. The audience has to take as much of the responsibility for evaluation as the performer or presenter. They must learn to sort truth from opinion and the malicious from the critical.

In the past, dominant cultural groups made the rules, set the standards, and defined the norms, though this did not always ensure that the truth emerged. As we move into a culture that has both nonhierarchical networks, such as the Internet, and hierarchical networks, including television and newspapers, audience members must take on the role of arbiters of their own culture. One of the positive aspects of these changes is that each part of the cultural "theater" must become more responsible.

In his book *Laws of Form,* G. Spencer-Brown says that we are always at both ends of the telescope, both ends of any observation. Our eyes receive the light *from* the stars and process it, but our minds are also, in a sense, out *in* the stars, choosing, identifying, and composing what we see. As an audience, we have the responsibility to be as well trained as we can so that we can understand the messages and the relationships that are being sent to us.

Shakespeare composed his plays so that people who had no formal learning were laughing at the off-color jokes; at the same time, people who knew the history that the play was based upon were amused by the way the story was told. Simultaneously, the most sophisticated members of the audience were weaving together the whole experience: the ideas about the process of composing, the history that was being told, the quality of the acting, *and* the off-color jokes. They were also able to get more with subsequent experiences of the play. Because the physical layout of the Globe theater placed everyone around the stage, each member of the audience could enjoy the presence of others and share in the cultural richness of the experience. Seeing evidence that others were experiencing the play on different levels—some smiled, some cried, others whispered—was inspirational and provided a model for the less-involved theatergoers. The cultural event served to weave the audience together, establish criteria of excellence, and demonstrate the importance of the author, the actor, and the theater itself.

As the earth's population grows in size, as cultures expand or contract, and as the contexts of culture change, new authors and new cultural forms emerge. The greatness of some authors, artists, and inventors stays constant both because the educational system and the cultural system train people to be good audiences for their work—*and*, of course, because the work was superb, containing metaphors and ideas that are timeless. Shakespeare, for example, still continues as an example of greatness.

But why do many say there are no more authors in Shakespeare's league? Well, one answer is that he has become his own separate standard of excellence: We now have Shakespeare and everything that occurred before and after him. The audience has changed, too, as has the context in which his plays can be presented—and Shakespeare's work has *contributed* to those changes. More people are seeing and reading Shakespeare than ever before, but no one is composing as he did, in the way that he did, because the audience and the historical moment in which he composed have changed forever.

We are lucky audiences because we now get to experience not only the greatness of Shakespeare but also the array of people who have used his work as a standard of excellence. Current authors write both for the audience that they imagine *and* for the actual audience that arrives. Works of the past become part of the context for works in the present, and audiences that learn about the past become better audiences in the present.

For a work of art to be vital, it must become a lens through which our lives and our culture can be seen. The current array of lenses to choose from is astonishing, and the standards of comparison for today's artists are awesome. The opportunity to create with and for a contemporary audience is similar to the challenge that faced Shakespeare—but there is one crucial difference: Now the context includes the dizzying array of mass communication tools. The content of a work must be developed to relate to the context of these tools and what they have brought and cost us, or it won't find the audience it might deserve.

In Shakespeare's time, most people's lives were culturally closed compared to our own. They died within five miles of where they were born, and lived, on average, only thirty years. Today the larger social and physical spaces that we inhabit create audiences that may still be fragmented but are no longer physically isolated. As in the past, people are concerned about *their* part of the world, but they now see their place as a part of the global environment. People are concerned with *their* own cultural group, but they see it against the backdrop of the entire earth's population. Where once artists composed for people like themselves, they must now think of many different types of people as the audience for their ideas. It is important that artists seek to use the access to larger audiences as a way to improve knowledge and understanding and not only to entertain and sustain cultural numbness. Shakespeare's respect for his audience was demonstrated by the craft and care with which he constructed something for everyone and aspirations for all. The same words and actions were able to entertain a diverse audience and to engage them all in appreciating what was happening onstage as well as in the audience. Some contemporary artists, such as Jim Henson, created works that children are amused by, and adults find charming, and teachers find admirable. More artists need to strive for this.

Works that combine what is considered popular with aspirations for engaging and changing the society are rare and important. The play *1776* by Sherman Edwards and Peter Stone is an example of a popular work that contains ideas about individual responsibility and democracy that are challenging and important—and palatable—for the audience. Cultural events sometimes serve to remind us of who we are, not who we want to be. James Joyce always worried that culture was becoming an arm of the government, trying to control our dreams. Believing that collectively we can steer the right course means that artist and audience, producer and director, have the responsibility and challenge to make something great—by collaborating.

6

Museums and Public Places Provide a Context for Audiences to Develop

AFTER THE SECOND WORLD WAR, leisure time was created among the middle and lower classes as a by-product of changes in industry and commerce. Attendance at schools, colleges, and universities increased, and museums became interesting to this new audience, which was searching to learn and to improve themselves. Unfortunately, assumptions about the audience for which the museums were originally designed did not fit this new group. The new general public did not know about the history of many subjects and often did not have the educational background to discuss and integrate ideas that were being presented. As large and relatively informal spaces without the entry requirements and behavioral restrictions of formal classrooms, museums were perfect vehicles for introducing this audience to cultural ideas. However, since existing museums had, for the most part, been developed by scientists for the scientific voice in the culture, or by artists for the art history voice, or by historians for the dominant cultural voice, the metaphors of the place needed to be reinvented.

In 1970, when I designed my first museum, the Brooklyn Children's Museum, it seemed that what was needed was a new kind of experientially based exhibit that functioned more like a laboratory. The goal was to enable children and adults to learn about the world and their culture through play. Play is an effective way to teach, one that is not used nearly as much as it should be, and I counted on using it as the means to communicate. To get people to play at the Brooklyn Children's Museum, the environment needed to feel as if it *belonged* to the visitors. The audience had to *decide* how they wanted to explore it; they couldn't simply be told. The museum needed to be a new kind of place that welcomed its audience, showing them that they were respected, that they could learn, and that their ignorance was not a burden but actually an asset to the experience.

Fortunately, I was unaware of many of the

implications of the design I was proposing. None of the words that are part of our current vocabulary—*interactive, participatory, computer-controlled,* and so on—were in use then, so it was an adventure just to *define* the design, much less reach acceptance. As in all things, a small group carried the project to fulfillment: a supportive director, the chairman of the board, and an architect, all of whom knew, although probably not verbally, that a new paradigm was needed.

I wanted the Brooklyn Children's Museum to be like an eccentric aunt's garage into which people could go and, looking over the shoulder of their aunt, use the available tools to understand the world. I wanted it to be a model of how one could learn from the world by experimenting with it. The idea was for it to be a set of tools with which people could experiment—interacting with one another as well as with the museum itself—rather than artifacts that were perceived as being more valuable than the children experimenting. I wanted it to be like an ideal laboratory where the world could be explored and where cultural themes, both common and rare, could be examined. The aim was to eliminate any intermediary between the children and their process of exploration.

In the museum, the lighting and the structures are all used as tools for understanding, rather than simply being decorative. Just as a good conversation affects all the people talking, the physical museum should be responsive to the interests of the children as the children become interested in the museum. Each gesture toward exploration is met with a response and a transformation. I think of the museum as a learning environment, but that environment changes according to the activities of the children.

As you walk into the Brooklyn Children's Museum you see a huge ramp running down for a hundred yards. In it is a three-foot-wide stream. The stream provides water to other levels and exhibits, but it is also a place to sail toy boats. It *also* operates a small electric generator. Surrounding the ramp is a huge corrugated cylindrical drainpipe with neon lights circling within it. Children can also crawl through a transparent model of a carbon atom enlarged to many million times normal scale. They can investigate the entire museum before they decide what to play with.

Each level is devoted to one of the four basic elements into which people have historically and intuitively divided the physical world—earth, air, fire, and water. The water connects every level.

There is a fire level with a steam engine; the steam it produces can be used to run several different devices. The air area has a windmill, a pump elevator, and a compressor to inflate things; the earth level has an archaeological display and a small greenhouse.

One of the most valuable lessons I learned from my work on the Brooklyn Children's Museum was that when creating a museum, there are other relationships than just the one between the designer and the audience. The tools I designed had to complement the strength of the staff who would work at the museum after the designs and the construction were completed (and the designer no longer present). The cultural context of the "theater" itself had to be understood. I saw first-hand that in order to establish standards, one must look at the initial goals, then consider how close the work comes to achieving those goals. My initial aspiration was that children could be both actors and audience, and that the museum and the exhibits could be both theater and tools with which to create the experience. Looking back at how the Brooklyn Children's Museum, the first interactive museum, has endured in the years since my design was installed, I believe that the results were reasonably close to the goal.

WHEN SETTING STANDARDS, ANOTHER element must be considered: time. Any new institution needs time to create its audience and to become understood and included in the audience's set of important experiences. As an institution becomes part of a person's world, the ideas it conveys become part of that world, too, and part of what that person thinks and wants to do. Institutions, like museums, form the context, the theater in which and through which society and its cultures can converse. Institutions enable a diverse audience to have common experiences that give them not only the resources and a sense of belonging, but also the background ideas and information that enable them to further develop themselves and their individual roles in the culture.

The diversity of interest and experience in the audience is a resource if it can be channeled within a context that adds to each of our individual experiences and to the total range of our cultural experience. Institutions, especially museums, are uniquely positioned to provide the context where this communication can happen.

As we grow in number and add to the examples of excellence in different forms, we need to provide footprints so that new audiences can learn by experiencing excellent works at increasing levels of complexity. Just as we have children's books at several developmental levels—for early learners as well as more advanced ones—adults need to understand that simpler, more obvious stories and experiences also lead *them* toward more sophisticated ones. The footprints in any expressive form—from painting to music—are those works that are excellent but simpler to understand. Part of the development of a better audience is the development of the respect that needs to be shown for those who are first learning the basic elements of a cultural form. Museums are perfect places for this process of introduction and development to take place. The public should not be burdened by their ignorance and intimidated into refusing to enter into the experience. The communication design must express the idea that the audience's curiosity and unfamiliarity are why the exhibition was created.

Objective criteria of excellence function to help members of a culture choose the best from the enormous array of material being presented. In this sense, *objective* now means that many people agree to the criteria. In the past, *objective* usually meant the criteria of the dominant group within a society. For example, the objective criteria for the best music referred only to classical music. Refined further within that category, the best music was considered to have been composed by Bach. But as various ethnic and cultural communities have increased in size, education, and social power, these communities seek to explore other forms of expression to establish their own criteria as objective. Bach is no longer the only standard to which other composers are held.

The risk when change happens is that in the midst of developing new objective criteria, some earlier and valuable art forms can get overlooked or dismissed. This contributes to the sense that many have that valuable artistic expressions are being lost. But this can be overcome through museums and the Internet and all the multimedia databases that are being developed. Being able to join a music society on the Internet that is interested in an obscure French composer (without having to demonstrate prowess in the field), or going to a small recital of lute music at an institution and finding a relatively active group who share a sense of value with and appreciation of this music, replaces the need for *everyone* to share the same appreciation. Information and communication tools that are accessible to a very broad audience enable that audience to choose, develop, and grow at thousands of different levels. Exclusion ceases to become a principal need of the larger culture, since there are now so many venues and so many people who can attend. Being included, becoming part of an audience, will be a less intense, less difficult process that anyone can access, independent of his or her level of achievement, economic situation, or even physical location. The ultimate goal is to create new contexts in which many different art forms can be experienced, evaluated, and appreciated. Appreciating Bach should complement an appreciation of Bob Dylan and not exclude it—and vice versa.

THE CHICAGO SYMPHONY ORCHESTRA is an extraordinary institution in this regard. Constantly seeking to develop and enhance its audience through experimental discussion groups and adventuresome selections of music, the orchestra is broadening the range of music to be objectively valued as excellent. Recently the Chicago Symphony Orchestra wanted to reach out to involve more of the community in that process. Symphony leaders felt that classical symphonic orchestral music was not appealing to many communities in Chicago (or elsewhere, for that matter). They recognized that the music has long been associated with wealthy and aristocratic communities while being ignored by others. They asked themselves why. Some of the questions that came up were: Is it the music itself that is not valid? Is it the audience that is flawed? Is it that the sounds are not attractive? Is the experience in the concert hall not beautiful? Is it that people don't come because they do not feel comfortable being part of the audience? Or is it something else entirely?

Working with the Chicago Symphony Orchestra to try to make new audiences aware of the excellence of the institution and the music, I decided that I would try to change both people's preconceived perception of who the audience *is* for this music, and their perception of what the actual *music* is. The first step was to design an attractive space with an entrance that was inviting to the broadest possible range of people. Before anything could possibly happen in a musical sense, I had to get the audience inside. The entrance had to welcome a whole new audience; it had to convey the message that *anyone* could be there. Then I decided to look for reasons why the earlier dominant cultural groups *liked* classical symphonic music, why they wanted to pass it down to the next generation and share it with their peers. I hoped I might find an attractive set of ideas that *everyone* might want to try.

Ultimately, I identified five ideas that seemed to be the structural center points of classical music's appeal. The first was the idea of *teamwork*. Orchestras are extraordinary repositories of teamwork—the results of that group effort can be instantly seen, experienced, and appreciated, and the aesthetic of that teamwork, when successful, is extraordinary.

The second idea was *sound*. We needed to explore the way in which sound was being produced, then how to judge and assess it.

The third idea was *ritual and celebration*. Music weaves our culture together and is always part of rites of passage and seasonal and religious holidays. At every concert, whether it is jazz, rock, or classical, people dress up to heighten the experience of being in the event together. This tells us that music plays a crucial role in creating and sustaining our connection to each other and to the cycles in the physical and metaphysical world.

The fourth idea was the idea of *metaphors and links*. It is always interesting to learn to associate one sensory idea with another, different sensory idea. For example, we often see colors as emotions, images as stories, pictures as textures, and sound as having meaning. There are great examples in classical symphonic orchestral music, like Verdi's *Otello* or *Falstaff*, where composers have used stories as the underlying metaphor for a piece of music. This kind of music allows us the chance to integrate our senses through the experience.

The fifth idea was about *mapping and notation*. A complex piece of music cannot be performed by a group of people until it is written down. Once that is done, any group can attempt the piece, and by comparing performances, either live or on recordings, musicians in one group can learn from other orchestras. Also, it is nearly impossible to create new audiences without teaching music or listening to music outside of a live performance. The ability to record and write down music, then play it back, allows musicians to improve their performances, to create an array of all kinds of music, and to use it to expand and enhance our understanding about the ways in which music is made around the world.

After such conceptualizing, the next step was

to turn the concept into something physical—
something that actually *works*. The facility I designed to present this is called ECHO. As the
visitors to ECHO arrive, they can choose one of
four boxes shaped like instruments that they will
use as their interface for the upcoming experience.
Each box is based on one of the four basic instru-
ment types: air—like a trumpet, vibration—like a
xylophone, membrane—like a drum, or string—
like a violin. Each box has a design like that instru-
ment that enables visitors to play it as they engage
in the experience and a memory chip that records
what they do. Each of the five ideas—teamwork,
sound, ritual and celebration, metaphors and links,
mapping and notation—is presented at a separate
enclosed console that looks a little like a phone
booth. The visitors use their box at each console to
explore one of the concepts. What they create at
each console is recorded in the box, and after they
have visited each of the five consoles, they can take
their box and put it on a shelf on the Orchestral
Wall. There they hear a composition of which their
creative efforts become one part.

The overall intent is not dissimilar to the intent
of the Indonesian shadow-puppet play. Visitors to
ECHO are able to examine music from all angles.
They are *inside* the creation as well as *observers* of

the creation. They are not just *taught* the concept of music; they are able to *play* with the central themes of the music, becoming comfortable and having the opportunity to experience the joy of being an audience. Once that happens, perhaps they can then see how music is relevant to and can enliven their lives.

Instead of trying to make musicians of the visitors, my goal was to make them into a great audience, one that understands why classical symphonic orchestral music has been preserved at great cost by previous generations. Because they are learning interactively, the possibility is increased that they will develop *beyond* the audiences that currently attend the symphony. It is my hope that new standards of excellence will be created not by the performers alone but by the audience, performers, and the context together.

M OST ENTERTAINMENT AND MUSEUM experiences are not designed to engage the visitor in anything more than passive wonder. Such displays and spectacles do not engage visitors in conversation but simply "lecture" them about a particular idea. The drawback to this approach is that if visitors do not have any existing context into which to fit the new idea, the lecture is usually ignored.

Some designers try to lure audiences by telling a mythlike story that includes overwhelming special effects and makes full use of intense sound, speed, and imagined danger. But this only distracts people by giving them a sensation of "safe" danger. Going to a theme park, especially a Disney theme park, is a clear example of how this works. Roller coasters and fantasy abound, but nothing dirty, nothing bad, nothing that violates dominant social values, is ever at risk of being seen when participating in a Disney theme-park experience. The audience experience at a Disney theme park has nothing to do with the reality of being there; visiting such a place is merely a way to express membership in the values of society.

The all-important conversation with the audience and supporting conversations within the audience are not enhanced at all by these theme-park experiences. People tend not to talk to others outside their own group. Even families tend not to discuss ideas themselves; at best, they merely respond to external stimuli. Everything is *provided* during the visit. There is nothing left for the family to provide. It is done brilliantly, but underneath the gloss, these theme parks do nothing to prepare people for the complex changing and demanding roles of people in the twenty-first century. It is a moment of nostalgia for the simple story life told in the movies, posing as an active experience. It is also an experience that is filled with messages about the integration of business and corporate identity into daily life.

The Disney theme-park experience can certainly be fun, but that kind of experience can be satisfying and extend our standards of excellence only if it is mixed with experiences enabling one to question and experience a dynamic and active role in the culture in which we live.

WHEN I START ON a project, I tell my clients that they have to choose: They can try to transfer lots of information about the ideas or products that they are interested in, or they can create an exhibit that makes the visitor smarter so that he or she can become a more active, interested, and questioning audience for the ideas or product. If we are to use available technology to raise the standards of our society, exhibits must engage the audience so that they are better able to make up their own minds and choose to use, think about, or be influenced by the idea being presented. Like the experience of the shadow puppets, being engaged and being invited to be engaged in all aspects of an event opens people's eyes to the possibility of their involvement in the experience. If an event includes all aspects of preparation and development rather than working from one vantage point only, that of staying in the theater seat, for example, then the choice of which element of the production to be engaged with—the story, the characters, the music, or any other role or combination of roles—is left up to the audience.

With an authentic and meaningful role, the audience can experience the value of community. For so long, we have modeled ourselves to fit into a culture where individual success is the measure of social success. Now we must expand the model to include collective success, with communal roles and responsibilities an important part of our value structure. An audience that experiences a cultural event in a fully engaged manner, involved with the performance and with each other, can be an important element in this new world.

To communicate the value of being in such an audience requires not only well-crafted experiences; it requires an audience that is open and eager to learn and expand their abilities. It is not inevitable that every audience will be attracted to more interactive experiences, especially when aspects of the interaction require or expect that members of the audience will prepare and learn and be curious and eager to explore. To assist the interactive quality of experiences, to complement this more intuitive strategy of learning, there needs to be access to learning that is more traditional in its approach and more goal-oriented. Goal-oriented learning, which is used to teach subjects like mathematics and foreign languages, is based on the idea of explaining the skill and the content as being intertwined and requiring focused individual practice and evaluation. Our ability to participate with others requires that we have a general level of common words, ideas, and models of thought that we can share to build a more complex understanding. Without participating in goal-oriented study, the more intuitive experiences that interactive learning usually employs can become inaccessible for a large part of the society. Computers, which assist in mass communication, can also assist in bringing the tools for goal-oriented learning to a large audience. It would be as confusing to suggest that all learning could take place experientially and interactively as it used to be to suggest that all learning should be presented in a goal-oriented style. It is the combination of the two styles, presented with the appropriate content in each, that will create the best climate for learning and culture.

IN MY WORK, I try to enable audiences to be more aware of, more in control of, and more excited by what they *think* in public places. Above all, I want the experiences I design to enhance the appreciation of others—both those in the room and those with whom one is communicating. There are approximately 238,000 more people on earth every day. Out of necessity, we must become more adept at, interested in, and appreciative of the value of working in large groups. Every experience that is designed for a public place must strive to enable people to appreciate, respect, and learn from and with those around them. The faster the population grows, the more difficult the public design process becomes—but the more we must strive to improve upon it. Designing as if we were back in a proscenium world or the mythic world of a Disney theme park is irresponsible. It ignores the needs of the present, which can only harm our future. To the degree that we do not increase everyone's participation and consider everyone's abilities in our plans for public experiences, we will only degrade their world and therefore our own. As each person is considered and included in the audience and as the audience learns from each other and about new ideas, each and every person can become a *contributor* to the quality of life. It is through this process that the standards of excellence become simultaneously inclusive and socially responsible.

Group public experiences must enable the participants to play and learn from one another as well as from the ideas presented. The design of an interactive public experience must anticipate the audience's resistance to join in; it must create tools that engage as a way of overcoming any resistance.

In Sesame Place, a small-scale theme park outside of Dallas, Texas, I learned that the public did not want to bring their children somewhere that presented ideas about science in such a way that might reveal their own lack of knowledge. In other words, you can't embarrass the adults. They don't want their children asking questions they can't answer. The solution, in this instance, was for Sesame Place to provide dignified study notes printed on posters. These were sent out to families all over the region as well as placed near the exhibits within the park so that the parents could answer the questions and feel prepared. This provides a way for adults to give themselves and their children permission to play and learn—and that is critical to the success of any design. Science has been and continues to be a challenging subject to integrate into the public dialogue. Tools must be created that enable people to play with scientific subjects without being burdened or embarrassed by their ignorance. Only by trying to change the relationship between a scientific presentation and the audience can that be achieved.

I always start the design process by asking myself who the visitors imagine themselves to be. Then I decide what the messages and themes are that the institution wants to tell them. At the Fernbank Museum of Natural History in Atlanta, Georgia, I wanted the visitor to be an amateur naturalist walking through both Georgia *and* geological history at the same moment. At the Kennedy Space Center, I wanted them to feel like citizens who were getting a briefing about what NASA has done and what its plans are for the future.

Often, scientists and museum staff get trapped in the language and the rules of their discipline and create exhibits that are exclusive rather than inclusive. That is one of the oldest problems of museums. How can the effort to understand something be rewarded except by excluding those who don't? The answer to that conundrum is that as the audience gets better it can make greater demands on the professionals to communicate better. Controlling the information flow only leads to controlled ignorance. Fortunately, it is possible to let many voices work together to pose questions and solve problems through the Internet and other nonhierarchical information channels. But we still need to create public places where science can be explored through play. More of us need to share in the awe and wonder of understanding how the world works. As more information becomes available, more people will be encouraged to assemble routes through and links within the body of data. Standards of database excellence will emerge, as will theses about what information means. Standards arise from knowledge *and* from need. The extraordinary communications tools we have to-day must be used not just to expedite the flow of information but also to assemble patterns within it that enhance its use.

HENRY FORD, A GREAT inventor of process—consider the assembly line—was obsessed with invention and the need for it. In a twelve-acre building in Dearborn, Michigan, he assembled a collection of some of the greatest inventions in history. Among them are the first engine ever made, in England in the twelfth century, and examples of the wide variety of washing machines invented in the United States in the 1930s. The museum also includes Thomas Edison's last breath, which is sealed in a glass vial. It is an amazing place. Ford wanted it to serve as a laboratory to a school he built to help train a new generation of inventors. The school no longer operates, but more than a million people visit the museum each year.

About eight years ago, the Ford Museum gave me a wonderful challenge. I was asked to design an experience that would help the public understand the idea of innovation and which would show the invention collection as an inspiring example of how innovation works to create great things in our culture. I decided to create something called the Innovation Station. It shows the visitors to the museum that all these tens of thousands of inventions did not arise in a void and were not only created by the individual inventors but are really the result of collaboration.

One of the core ideas of innovation is that the inventor does not really work in isolation but must work with others to solve problems and create. To allow the visitors to experience this, I created a huge machine that visitors could step into and learn to work together to make something happen. The machine I designed is a ball-sorting machine; it covers an area of four thousand square feet and needs thirty-five people to operate. Before the visitors start, a staff person explains that every innovation happens between people and that this Innovation Station will succeed to the degree that the people talk and work together to sort the different colored balls. Then each of the players gets into one of the thirty-five stations, and they all work together for twenty minutes to solve their problem. The stations have activities that range from exercise bicycles with several people trying to crank the balls up to the ceiling, to a large transparent sphere hanging overhead that the visitors turn to select which path the ball will flow through. It is one of the most successful interactive designs I have ever done, because it involves a group of visitors in a comprehensible experience that enables them to clearly perceive the value of the other visitors' contributions. It also lets them perceive the value of play. Proper interaction means that each person in the process is affecting the outcome. They are communicating their needs, which are being integrated into the whole experience. And that experience is comprehensible and accessible to everyone.

MOST INTERACTIVE DESIGNS ARE misnamed. They are not based on involving the audience in a compositional or collaborative experience. Instead they are built on the capabilities of the device or computer to put some simplified story in motion. There is usually some superfluous switch or button inserted to provide the *illusion* of involvement. Such devices point up the difference between an illustration and a real game. Inviting people to see an illustration simply makes them passive observers, even if they have to push a button to see it. Asking someone to join in a game, on the other hand, requires him or her to be involved in the experience. Interaction is the beginning of a relationship between the person participating, other people in the environment, and/or the person who composed the experience. A rich interactive experience is a game, like chess or Monopoly, in which the outcome of each move affects the overall experience.

A true test of whether something is interactive is to subtract the experience from the environment and see if anything happens. If the design is truly interactive, there will be nothing left, since the experience and the environment (the theater) are the same. The Innovation Station is *still* unless people are in it, making the balls circulate and trying to sort the different colored balls. At Hanna-Barbera Land in Houston there is an exhibit in which people hold hands. The more people who are holding hands, the brighter the lights of the exhibit become. If there is no interaction—if no one holds hands and touches the exhibit—then the exhibit and the area around it are dark. That not only is a perfect example of an interactive experience, it's an excellent metaphor for what interactive experiences provide.

7

Interacting in the Audience
Creates the Possibility of
True Excellence

COMPUTERS OFFER A UNIQUE contribution to
the education process—the ability to supple-
ment an experience with access to every level of
information about that experience. While looking
at a painting, visitors will eventually be able to access films about the artist and his other life, see
newspapers of those times, learn about the context
in which the painting was created, or hear about
the painting's influence on others. Children can
use computers to explore the Indonesian culture
and have an on-line conversation with children
from Indonesia. They can discuss how to set up a
shadow-puppet show and how to judge a good

one from a bad one. Once most people are able to use computers properly, the audiences will develop dramatically.

New media tools enable members of the audience to actively redefine, analyze, and express their ideas in relation to an idea or experience. No longer will only experts be able to voice an opinion. There are always people who have never heard of some idea, just as there are always people for whom this idea is the center of their life; then, of course, there is the range of people in between. Opening up an experience to all three categories of authentic involvement, choice, and responsibility creates a climate in which excellence begins to be measured in the standards, aspirations, and desires of the audience rather than only those of the actors. Remembering the Balinese statement "We have no art. We do everything well" reminds us that when people's differing skills and roles are welcomed in a society, they can then assemble into different and interesting audiences or actors for cultural activity. Perhaps more important, they can also demand responsible actions from community members.

TODAY, REPETITION IS EQUATED with importance but disconnected from excellence. In
the past, high visibility of an idea could be inter-
preted as an expression on the part of cultural
leaders and others that this idea, this person, or
this thing was important for all of us. In our current society, seeing someone or something repeat-
edly can simply be an advertising strategy. It can
also be the result of a temporary cultural obsession
or the desire of publishers or broadcasters to create a wave of interest in some event that they
can cover. But we as the audience cannot detect
whether repetition means that we all think something is great or whether some organization wants
that image to be seen everywhere so that products
will sell.

When values dissociate from emphasis, the first
response is confusion. As this dissociation continues, the audience can have one of two additional
responses: It can become more astute in the choice
of things repeated, or it can become overstimulated
and numb. As we spend more time in our contemporary, media-rich, information-dense environment,

it becomes harder for us to determine whether people who own lots of recognizable things are valued more than people who do more valuable things with and for others. The hope is that as the audience improves and assumes more responsibilities for what they are watching and participating in, perhaps it will again become important to be judged by our actions, our friends, and ourselves, rather than by the brand of our possessions.

BEFORE THERE WERE TEXTS and books, people could not study an idea except by memorizing and repeating it. There was a rich oral tradition of speaking stories and poems and a well-trained aural culture that heard what it knew. Published books enabled people to read an expressed thought over and over again. In the early days of the printed word, a book had to last through many readings. So the audience, small as it was to begin with, cherished the book and pored over it for years, looking for different meanings and interpretations. The Bible and the complex late-sixteenth-century metaphysical poetry of John Donne are examples of works that continue to challenge readers to discover varied levels of interpretation.

As books became more readily available, education created more readers. As records of thought multiplied, the need for many levels of metaphors and meaning in one work became less important to the experience and desire of the audience. Most of the audience gradually and collectively forgot the oral/aural tradition; as a result, the audience stopped listening for complexity. People look to a succession of books, magazines, and newspapers—and now to movies and television—for *another* story and *another* idea to think and *another* thing to do. Poetry, which is built on many-layered aural experiences, has become a less appreciated art. In turn, vividness and easy assimilation have become more suited to an audience's desire. The experience of holding the words before you and having your eyes move across the words is no longer perceived as part of the event—reading is now more like a private talk with a person (the author) rather than realizing the complex process of communicating through symbol as an important aspect of what is communicated.

When films were shown exclusively in palace-type theaters, many metaphors, fears, and desires emerged from the experience of sitting in a big dark room with others having a powerful, shared, mythlike experience. A film was an event with a potentially huge impact, an experience that could envelop our entire being. And that experience was greatly heightened, since it was perceived to be a one-time thing—once the movie's run was over, we wouldn't see it again. As television appeared, films began to be recycled. In a living room, the grandeur of *Gone with the Wind* becomes like a postcard from the original experience.

Videocassettes are compressing this experience even more. Now our children see the mythic films and programs over and over again. They don't often share the experience of knowing and feeling the way a whole audience responds to things. They can watch something so often that its story and its meaning become strictly information, separate from the mystery of the intended emotion. Because of this repetition of simple, mythic stories, and because of the loss of value placed on the aural tradition, the complex interwoven metaphors of the films of Welles or Godard or Bertolucci are not as valued as before.

We no longer think of films as a communal experience. Rather, they are just part of the array of media placed alongside television, the Internet, and more. The immediacy of the other media has distracted us from the perception of the movie experience. News, fears, myths, and stories are presented simultaneously and on any medium for any purpose. A war or a crime is often fictionalized and presented within the very same time frame as actual news appears about it. Films are increasingly based on real-life events—often with very little transformation, blurring the line with reality. We sometimes look to film the way we look to television or the Internet—to find out what is happening, not to hear larger-than-life iconic voices that want to tell us about the ways in which we could be living our lives.

This blurring of reality and story can be quite dangerous. But if we become aware of this, we as the audience can sort out what we see and begin to *search* for iconic, mythic stories within appropriate communal contexts. When the audience, the artists, and the developers of new media contexts can use media appropriately—where television can be a mass communication/distribution tool for news and events; where the Internet can be an audience-building, information-supplying network between its users; where film, museums, and theaters can serve as places where we get together to experience the important shared ideas and issues of our culture—the culture and the society can aspire to develop more interesting and appropriate standards of excellence.

Not only do we now have an amazing array of media delivery systems, we also have a huge, widely accessible archive of material from the arts, the sciences, and *every* other field of art and learning from which to draw. Thanks to small CD players and recordings, for example, the potential audience for Mozart's music is not only serious, orthodox, classical music experts who can attend an expensive concert, it's anyone eating lunch or driving down the road. What we have to actively seek and create are the shared audience experiences of a work. We need to create experiences that encourage an audience's instinct to try new works and participate in old works. With our new tools, we can also reexamine and reevaluate the forms and expression that are important to maintain at center stage and those that become important to small and large audiences everywhere.

The new Mozarts may not be the ones simply composing music. They may be those people who create a dynamic compositional experience that enables people to comprehend how music is made, played, and understood. Excellence in interactive experience must be measured by the degree of conversation and transformation that occurs in the environment and the degree to which there is a shared sense that everyone is part of the process. Without an understanding of who the audience is, how they will work together, and how they will understand the roles that they will play, interaction can't work. The process of design always needs to anticipate the audience. It's the exact same process as when you invite people to your house—you cook the kind of food that you know they will like, but at the same time you try to expand their culinary horizons. It is a gradual educational process. The mass public does not yet know how to participate in interactive experiences, so interactive experiences have to explain not only how they work but what their ingredients are and how visitors can get the most out of them. It is essential to clearly state the rules, roles, and expectations of the experience at the outset, giving everyone equal footing on which to learn and participate.

If we are to keep our standards high—and even raise them—it is essential that interactive activities exclude as few people as possible. Composing interactive experiences has to be thought of as a collective composition involving *all* the voices and talents that have to be arrayed to create the experience and conversation that will eventually exist. Composing an interactive experience *first* requires the integration of the different parts of the audiences, then the addition of the different parts of the composed material: music, voice, content, interface, and so on.

It is easy to fail when designing an interactive experience. Designs fail when the designers do not know the audience, integrate the threads of content and context, welcome the public properly, or make clear what the experience is and what the audience's role in it will be.

At the moment, multiperson interactive experiences are rare. Some of the multiple-user domains and other Internet-based experiences are truly interactive and are contributing to a new standard of excellence—but the vast majority, like MYST, while great puzzle-solving experiences, do not really elicit group participation or collective composition. We cannot expect the audience for multiperson interactive experiences to develop until there are environments where people who are not familiar with or comfortable with computer technology can physically get together without being embarrassed by their unfamiliarity with computers. People must be given an opportunity to experiment with and experience multiplayer participatory games in person before they can effectively play in an electronic neighborhood. The Internet, as it is now used, creates electronic communities and isolation—even though its structure and intent is to link people. It is essential that we use the Internet to link voices, but we must also strive to create experiences that strengthen physical and emotional communities. That balance can then support a stable, heuristic, and benevolent culture. But it will take a conscious effort to make this happen. It is not inevitable.

FOR AN EXISTING SYSTEM to stay alive, the long-term goals of the whole system must not become subsumed by the short-term goals. In other words, *parts* of the system cannot dominate the whole. In every living system the primary goal is to stay alive. With our complex cultures and increasing population, we need experiences that provide models of how to make communities that thrive and in which individuals are also protected. The health of our system will rest on its ability to function while simultaneously placing no limits on the right to explore new ideas and maintaining the important basic rights for all. We need to beware of excessive control coming not only from the government but also from large corporations that try to control and limit access to the composition of information, media, and audience interaction.

T ODAY WE ARE OVERWHELMED by choice. The number of choices of media, and of the content in those media, is growing incredibly rapidly. The audience for each of these media—and for all the discrete communication strategies, art forms, language conventions, and affinity groups found in them—changes like the weather. As a result, more people than ever before can choose to realize their own ideas, not at the *expense* of others, but with their *assistance*. Art and communication can, with these choices, look toward the possibility of making great audiences that will demand great work from artists. If that work comes, it will continually challenge the audience to learn more, become more integrated, interesting, and interested, and in turn demand even greater work.

So why is it that people are not flocking to work together and develop and expand interactive experiences? Part of the answer is that we are creatures who learn through play, and our play has been directed toward individual achievement, toward becoming isolated from one another. Such isolation is often equated with power. The celebrity press is full of images of moguls and stars on their vast ranches, on their private jets, or standing alone at the top of their skyscrapers. We need to play in such a way and in such circumstances that allow us to see and create models of behavior in which large groups learn from and work with others to succeed. This play is not a replacement for individual success; it's a necessary complement to it. New inventions do not replace the old; rather, they improve aspects of them. Western culture has too often created models of success based on exclusion. We now must complement that with models based on inclusion. Interactive experiences by definition include people. Well-designed interactive experiences include *more and more* people. Excellence of the art now must be balanced by excellence of the audience. The context, the theater, must be expanded to include the development of a great, varied, and increasingly demanding audience.

There is only one protection against one dominant person or corporation or government controlling the context: The audience must expect and demand a rich and involved voice in the composition of the process. That is the lesson learned from the shadow puppets. The audience can learn from one another on the Internet, drawing information from large databases in order to discuss and evaluate events and ideas. They can compare performances recorded in the past with current ones and critique them. Audience interest in themes that connect and inspire us will create expectations for more. As we move into the next century, the most compelling performances, dramas, and ideas will be the ones that raise important issues between the members of the audience and that stimulate awareness and respect both *within* audiences and *between* them.

As an audience evolves, there are fundamental dichotomies and ironies that arise. Increased access to bodies of knowledge produces an increase in awareness of what there is *to* know—and therefore an increase in what is unknown. Direct multidirectional communication between people that does not need to be routed or translated through a controlling, dominant media force creates an awareness of others that is less abstract, more reliable, and more dependable than the unidirectional communication of, say, television. Therefore, respect and awareness of others becomes more possible. An increase in the culture's acknowledgment of interdependence creates an increase in interdependence. Once people know that they can, should, and *must* depend on one another, they begin to develop the means, behaviorally, linguistically, and technologically, to do just that.

The measurement of the success of these new communication patterns will become a new measure of excellence in the society. But we must keep in mind that excellence is a changeable measure, and because it changes there are moments in our history when society seems to have lost the ability to control the definition. Lately these moments have come because of the enlargement of the audience, the increase in the number of points of view that are expressed, and the staggering increase in the number of channels of information. This stage will be short if we are able to pay attention to these changes and develop strategies to integrate the difference and respect the new voices in our society.

WITH YOUR UNAIDED EYES you can look into a pond and see clear water. With a magnifying glass you look into the same water and see thousands of small organisms. With a microscope you see bacteria and detect viruses, and with the most sophisticated tunneling electron microscope you can see the atoms that make up the water and the creatures in it. Each level of magnification enables us to compose a story about what we are seeing and then relate it to other levels of observation. Eventually this process affects our decision to take a swim. The more we are aware of our role in each level of observation, perception, and conception, the more we become responsible for our success and can truly enjoy the entire show of our lives.

Our future relies on our ability to create great teams of artists and audiences, broadcasters and critics, observers and creators. Each of these groups wants the audience to be better, because that's the only way we can be assured that the show will improve. It is the resonance between the audience and the show—all elements of the event—that creates greatness in each. Excellence exists only in the variety and quality of our interactions.

Bibliography

Axelrod, Robert. *The Evolution of Cooperation*. New York: Basic Books, 1985.

Bacon, Francis. *Novum Organum; with Other Parts of the Great Instauration*. Translated and edited by Peter Urbach and John Gibson. Chicago: Open Court, 1994.

Bateson, Gregory. *Steps to an Ecology of Mind: Collected Essays in Anthropology, Psychiatry, Evolution, and Epistemology*. Northvale, NJ: Jason Aronson, 1987.

Bell, Daniel. *The Coming of Post-Industrial Society: A Venture in Social Forecasting*. New York: Basic Books, 1976.

Bellah, Robert N. *Habits of the Heart: Individualism and Commitment in American Life*. Berkeley and Los Angeles: University of California Press, 1985.

Bruce, Robert V. *Bell: Alexander Graham Bell and the Conquest of Solitude*. Ithaca, NY: Cornell University Press, 1990.

Cannon, Walter B. *Wisdom of the Body*. New York: Norton, 1963.

Carpenter, Edward. *Intermediate Types among Primitive Folk: A Study in Social Evolution.* New York: Arno Press, 1975.

Cassirer, Ernst. *Essay on Man: An Introduction to a Philosophy of Human Culture.* New Haven and London: Yale University Press, 1992.

Clifford, James. *The Predicament of Culture: Twentieth-Century Ethnography, Literature and Art.* Cambridge: Harvard University Press, 1988.

Colinvaux, Paul A. *Why Big Fierce Animals Are Rare: An Ecologist's Perspective.* Princeton, NJ: Princeton University Press, 1988.

Fuller, Buckminster. *Operating Manual for Spaceship Earth.* Mattituck, NY: Amereon, 1978.

Gardner, Howard E. *Frames of Mind: The Theory of Multiple Intelligences.* New York: Basic Books, 1993.

Goffman, Erving. *The Presentation of Self in Everyday Life.* New York: Anchor, 1959.

Hall, Edward Twitchell. *The Silent Language.* New York: Anchor, 1973.

———. *The Hidden Dimension.* New York: Anchor, 1990.

Lippmann, Walter. *The Public Philosophy.* New Brunswick, NJ: Transaction, 1989.

Marcuse, Herbert. *One Dimensional Man: Studies in the Ideology of Advanced Industrial Society.* New York: Farrar, Straus and Giroux, 1964.

Margulis, Lynn. *Microcosmos: Four Billion Years of Evolution from Our Microbial Ancestors.* Berkeley and Los Angeles: University of California Press, 1997.

Maturana, Humberto R. *Autopoiesis and Cognition: The Realization of the Living.* Boston: D. Reidel, 1980.

McCulloch, Warren S. *Embodiments of Mind.* Cambridge: MIT Press, 1988.

McHale, John. *The Future of the Future.* New York: George Braziller, 1969.

McLuhan, Marshall. *Understanding Media: The Extensions of Man.* New York: Mentor/New American Library, 1964.

Minsky, Marvin. *The Society of Mind.* New York: Simon and Schuster, 1988.

Monod, Jacques. *Chance and Necessity: An Essay on the Natural Philosophy of Modern Biology.* New York: Random House, 1972.

Ong, Walter J. *Orality and Literacy: The Technologizing of the Word.* London and New York: Routledge, 1982.

Ortega y Gassett, José. *The Revolt of the Masses.* New York and London: W.W. Norton, 1994.

Piaget, Jean. *Origins of Intelligence in Children.* New York: International Universities Press, 1992.

Popper, Karl R. *Conjectures and Refutations: The Growth of Scientific Knowledge.* London and New York: Routledge, 1992.

Schlesinger, Arthur M. *Cycles of American History.* Boston: Houghton Mifflin Company, 1987.

Shakespeare, William. *The Complete Works.* General editor, Alfred Harbage. Baltimore, MD: Penguin, 1969.

Sherrington, Charles. *Man on His Nature.* Cambridge: Cambridge University Press, 1985.

Slater, Philip Elliot. *Pursuit of Loneliness: American Culture at the Breaking Point.* Boston: Beacon Press, 1990.

———. *The Glory of Hera: Greek Mythology and the Greek Family.* Princeton, NJ: Princeton University Press, 1992.

Spencer-Brown, G. *Laws of Form.* New York: Julian Press, 1972.

Stein, Gertrude. *How to Write.* New preface and introduction by Patricia Meyerowitz. New York: Dover Publications, 1975.

Thompson, D'Arcy Wentworth. *On Growth and Form.* New York: Dover Publications, 1992.

Tocqueville, Alexis de. *Democracy in America.* New York: New American Library, 1991.

Turnbull, Colin M. *The Forest People.* New York: Simon and Schuster, 1972.

———. *The Mountain People.* New York: Touchstone Books, 1987.

Whitehead, Alfred North. *Process and Reality.* New York: Free Press, 1985.

Whorf, Benjamin Lee. *Language, Thought and Reality.* Cambridge: MIT Press, 1956.

Wittgenstein, Ludwig. *Tractatus Logico Philosophicus.* London and New York: Routledge, 1981.

Young, John Z. *Doubt and Certainty in Science: A Biologist's Reflections on the Brain.* Westport, CT: Greenwood, 1982.

About the Author

EDWIN SCHLOSSBERG has a Ph.D. in science and literature from Columbia University. He is the author of *Einstein and Beckett: A Record of an Imaginary Conversation, The Philosopher's Game, The Home Computer Handbook, The Pocket Calculator Game Book, The Pocket Calculator Game Book #2,* and *The Kid's Pocket Calculator Game Book.* He founded Edwin Schlossberg Incorporated (ESI), a multidisciplinary design firm that has specialized in exhibit and interactive design for public places for over twenty years. Dr. Schlossberg lives in New York City with his family.

A Note on The Library of Contemporary Thought

This exciting new monthly series tackles today's most provocative, fascinating, and relevant issues, giving top opinion makers a forum to explore topics that matter urgently to themselves and their readers. Some will be think pieces. Some will be research oriented. Some will be journalistic in nature. The form is wide open, but the aim is the same: to say things that need saying.

Look for these titles coming soon from
The Library of Contemporary Thought

ANNA QUINDLEN
HOW READING CHANGED MY LIFE

WILLIAM STERLING AND STEPHEN WAITE
BOOMERNOMICS
Technology, Globalization, and the Future of Your
Money in the Upcoming Generational Warfare

JIMMY CARTER
THE VIRTUES OF AGING